MADAM VELVET'S
Cabaret of Oddities

Nancy Stohlman

ISBN: 978-1-945917-45-5

Printed in the United States of America

Front Cover Artwork: Susan Ryplewski

Also by Nancy Stohlman:

The Vixen Scream and Other Bible Stories
The Monster Opera
Fast Forward: The Mix Tape(editor)
Searching for Suzi: a flash novel
Fast Forward: A Collection of Flash Fiction Vol II (editor)
Fast Forward: A Collection of Flash Fiction Vol I (editor)

 BIG TABLE
Publishing

"Making other books jealous since 2004"

Big Table Publishing Company
Boston, MA
www.bigtablepublishing.com

Versions of these stories have appeared in the following publications:

"Clown Car" *Funny Bone: Flashing for Comic Relief* anthology

"Traveling Medicine Show and "My Mother Was a Circus Clown" on Rocky Mountain Revival Podcast

"My Father is Trying to Set the World Record for Days Spent Petting a Shark"* *Blink Ink*

"The Man From the Future" *The Airgonaut*

"My Mother Was a Circus Clown" and "The Augmentation" *Flash: The International Short Story Magazine*

"The Dressing Room", "The Topless Bar", and "The Man from the Future" *Lost in Thought Magazine*

"Welcome to the Fantasy Hand Job Brothel" *The Incredible Shrinking Story* anthology

"The One Thing My Grandfather Won't Talk About" *Blink Ink*

"Interview with the Electric Lady" *Flash Frontier* as part of "People From our Pages"

"The Four-Legged Woman" *Pure Slush*

"The Fortune Teller" *Flash Frontier*

* Finalist for Vera Flash Fiction Award, *Vestal Review*, and nominated for a Pushcart Prize

for my mother, who taught me to be a clown
and for Dan, who made me join the circus

Table of Contents

MADAM VELVET'S
Cabaret of Oddities

Nancy Stohlman

The Dressing Room

I was staring in the mirror at my reflection when the manager came in and told me I was fired. You're fired, he said. You just don't look enough like Grace Slick anymore, he said. People are starting to get suspicious and they pay good money to see Grace Slick. Be out of the dressing room by the end of the day.

I had hoped his crush on me would override this reaction, but it did not.

I looked at my reflection after he left. What are we going to do now? I asked.

We could always go back to Illinois? she suggested.

I suppose we have no choice, I said. And then I broke the mirror and kept a piece, so I could take her with me.

The Man from the Future

I was in the bathroom unsuccessfully killing myself when the man from the future arrived. He must have noticed my hesitation, the colorful array of pills, the way I could not meet my reflection in the mirror.

Looks like I got here just in time, he said, stepping out of the shower.

How did you get into my shower? I asked, aware now that I was wearing no panties.

He held out an aerosol can. Instant Fame* it said in cursive script. He put it on the counter. By the way your future self says hello and don't open another credit card.

Instant Fame*

Are you having a difficult time getting famous? Do you tell yourself each year that this will be the year? Are your friends getting famous and you're not? Do you wish there was a shortcut?

Well now there is! Instant Fame* will do in minutes what used to take years, even decades. With just 1 squirt you will feel the effects—1-3 sprays for local fame, 5-7 for national fame and 8+ sprays for international fame. Don't wait another minute while someone else stands in your spotlight! Take charge of your future now!

The can had an old fashioned yellow nozzle. Instant Fame was written in pink cursive script surrounded by sparkly stars.

Do it, my reflection urged.

I aimed the spray at my face and pushed the nozzle. It was all pink smoke and smelled like cotton candy and it burned and made me sneeze.

Nothing is happening, she said.

Just give it a sec, I said.

The Taxi Driver

Hurry, I said as we mobilized, shoving shoes in a purse. Here, take these, I said, grabbing wilted flowers, and we ran up the back emergency stairs to street level and hailed a cab.

My reflection and I waited on the curb. The streets were filled with Amish people wearing wool skirts and starched hats and everything smelled like fabric softener. My reflection's sharp edges were cutting me through my pants pocket and I took her out to tell her so but she was just scowling at me so I didn't give her the satisfaction of actually looking at her.

The taxi was buttery and yellow. The driver was wearing a paper halo and wings. How much to take us to Illinois? I asked.

Twelve thousand dollars, he said.

The Topless Bar

I'd love to hire you, the manager said after my audition, but one of your legs is longer than the other.

I've never noticed that before.

Oh, everyone else notices, he said. You kinda wobble around lopsided up there. It makes the customers uncomfortable. They're afraid you're going to fall off the stage.

He went to his computer and pulled up a photo of the Leaning Tower of Pisa. Like that, he said. And frankly you make me uncomfortable too. It's a little unnerving if I'm truly honest.

I had no idea, I said, embarrassed.

In the Parking Lot of the Swingers Club

Are we really going in there? my reflection asked.

I watched scrubbed men with shiny bald heads get out of limos.

No, let's just forget it, I said.

At the Casino

You can't bring that mirror in here, the security guard said.

Behind the Carnival

Turn here, my reflection pointed. A dirt road full of potholes led to a big wooden fence.

Where are we?

We're behind the carnival, she said as I adjusted her in the rearview mirror. I know a guy who might give us work.

What can you do? he asked when we found his booth.

We don't know.

Can you make toys?

Maybe, I said. Depends on what kind.

What does that matter? This isn't Santa's workshop.

Maybe something else?

How are you at getting tomatoes thrown at your face? he said. I had a guy just quit and I need another face by two o'clock.

We'll do it, my reflection said before I snapped the compact mirror closed on her.

My Mother Was a Circus Clown

When she kissed me goodnight she left smudges of white paint on my cheeks. When I tried to ask her a question she was inside a box—a wall left, right, above, oh my! When I came home from school she was painting pink eyebrows on her forehead. When I tried to hug her she squirted me with a rubber flower or knocked herself unconscious with a rubber sledgehammer or blew confetti out of a trumpet.

It's because her parents never let her see live music when she was growing up, my father explained. It was against their religion or something. She vowed to become a clown if they didn't let her see Elvis when he came through town back in '76.

My mother nodded, miming a tear sliding down her cheek with her gloved hand.

A List of Sideshow Performers circa 1885

The Human Skeleton
The Armless Woman
The Elastic Man
The Human Torso
Jo-Jo, The Dogfaced Boy
The Siamese Twins
The Albino Family
The Giantess
The Snake Charmer
Boy With Breasts
Flip The Frog Boy
Stigmata Man
The Tattooed Man
Lobster Boy
The Strong Man
The Four-Legged Woman
The Long Haired Lady
The Electric Lady
Lion Faced Boy
Hen Without a Bill

The Four-Legged Woman

Jacqueline Hele'ne, the infamous four-legged woman, was born a dipygus—a rare form of conjoined twinning where one twin fuses with the lower half of the other and everything forms in duplicate—two pelvises, four legs, two sets of ovaries, two vaginas.

As a baby Jacqueline's father would let the neighbors look at her for a nickel. By the time she was 13 she had joined the largest traveling circus as "The Amazing Four-legged Girl," where she showcased her oddities for the next decade. Her act was so popular that by the time Jacqueline left the carnival, there were dozens of phony four-legged women in sideshows across the country.

Jacqueline eventually married and bore two babies from her right uterus and three from her left. Men who heard this news confirmed that she had a preference for the left side in other ways as well.

Alien Baptism

Pope Francis has announced that he will baptize an alien this coming Sunday. "To my knowledge it will be the first alien baptism on record," he said to reporters. "The Church is just ecstatic."

The alien, whose name and age are unknown, has adopted the Christian name Maurice. While the language barrier has reportedly been a factor, Pope Francis insists that Maurice has chosen Catholicism from an informed place in his heart.

When asked why he decided to perform the highly controversial baptism, Francis replied, "That is between Maurice and the Lord."

Maurice will be one of 52 baptisms being performed this Sunday. The ceremony will include full emersion for both children and babies. Crowds are expected to fill Vatican City and extra security is being employed.

Message in a Bottle

Dear Sir or Madam,

I am being held prisoner in the jungle and am writing this by flashlight with the sounds of dogs in the background, so forgive me if I make any mistakes of grammar. I have 1.1 MILLION DOLLARS in gold bars buried in the dirt of your country but I have no way to access it in my present situation. I am looking for someone to dig up the bars and convert them to the currency of your country and for that I will share the rewards 50/50. You must mail the gold bars to me wrapped in aluminum foil and then my funds will be spent to rebuild the orphanage as my wife and I are missionaries and she is also dying of malaria. I cannot dig myself because I lost both my arms in a terrible train accident—I am writing this letter using a stick between my teeth and I also fear I have just been poisoned so you must act quickly.

I await your response and your banking information!

The Strong Man

Can we borrow a shovel?

What do you need a shovel for? he asked. Planning to kill someone?

No, nothing like that, we said. Just want to do some digging.

Do you need help? he asked, handing us the shovel.

No, we got it, we said as we backed away.

The Time Capsule

The ground was dry and powdery. We dug until we hit something hard and silver.

It's a time capsule, I said. Mom and I buried it when I was a kid.

Inside were polka dotted ties, giant flyswatters, cups with red rubber foam balls, a giant foam/plastic hot dog with oversized pickles, squirting flowers, disappearing ink, a tiny finger guillotine, a giant pacifier and diaper and bonnet totally mangled beneath broken Emmett Kelly statuettes.

Did she mean to bury all this? my reflection asked.

Yes. I forgot until just now.

Clown Childhood

Hey, your mom's a clown a kid said to me on the school bus. She was at my little brother's day care. Does she take that makeup off at home?

Or does she still wear it because she's so ugly?

Someone laughed.

And then everyone laughed.

Clown Cigarettes

When I came home from school my mother was holding a pack of cigarettes and grinning. She held the pack out to me as if encouraging me to take one.

I'm nine, I said. She waited. When I didn't say anything else, she squeezed and a thin stream of water came shooting out of the end of the pack and hit my shirt.

She bent over laughing without any sound.

Operation

In a bizarre reversal of irony, Hal Brown, who invented the popular children's game "Operation" in the 1970s, has announced that he cannot afford his own operation.

The game, which mimicked such medical procedures as removing the funny bone, water on the knee, brain freeze, and the wishbone, jolted kids with an electrical shock when they failed. "I don't believe in sugar coating things," Brown said. "If you don't have patience and a completely steady hand then your patient is going to die on the operating table in front of you. Period."

The game was recalled and removed from shelves after it was linked to epileptic and grand mal seizures in both children and adults.

Faced with his own needed operation and corresponding lack of funds, he says it's in god's hands now.

Past Life Self

Myself in a past life pulled over to the side of the road in a horse-drawn carriage. Get in quickly she said, pulling a cloak over her head as the horses stomped impatiently.

What's going on? I asked.

These gentlemen are taking me to safety, she said, worriedly looking out of the curtains. People want to kidnap me and extort my father for money. She smoothed her red bustle; her breasts spilled from her bodice. What luck that I found you, she said. This affects you, too.

How so? I asked.

Oh, you'll be dealing with this for years, she said knowingly.

The Portrait

She looks so snotty, my reflection said, refusing to look at it. My Past Life Self was seated on an upholstered chair, turned slightly away from the artist, the layers of her French ruffled petticoat cascading to the edges of the frame. Do we really have to hang it in here?

I like it, I said.

I think she looks a little suspicious. And a little chunky, don't you think? she said.

French Twist

Oh hi, my reflection said in the morning as I pinned my hair into a perfect French Twist. She was wearing her hair the exact same way.

Hi, I said as I brushed my teeth, noticing that she had somehow acquired the exact same pink babydoll nightgown as me.

Nice nighty, I said.

Yours too, she said, looking away.

Ménage a Trois

Check this out, said The Ringmaster, dimming the lights—
there are mirrors on this ceiling.

I looked up and saw my reflection, naked and flushed and
waiting. She had shaved her pubes to look exactly like mine.

Oh wow, this was a great idea, he said, staring at her. It's
kinda like I'm having sex with two of you.

Which killed the mood for me, so I got dressed and left.

The Talent Scout

The talent scout pulled my reflection aside. I think you should consider it, he said, handing her a business card.

The Human Skeleton

Art Ward was a normal kid until the age of 14 when he began to rapidly lose weight. The doctors could not explain it, calling it some unknown wasting disease. As an adult, unable to keep a job, he finally joined the circus sideshow as The Human Skeleton.

Art was not the only Human Skeleton act but he was the most notorious. Known for his carousing and womanizing, he allegedly tried to leave the circus many times, but his gambling debts always forced him to return. At the time of his death he weighed 43 pounds.

Urgent Follow-Up Telegram

Dear Ma'am,

I am so sorry you found no gold bars at the location I specified and I would like to pay you for your troubles—I am also wondering if I can ask you an additional favor—I am suffering from the cancer disease and I am a prince but I have no family and there is a car I wish to purchase—I'm so happy to have someone I can trust and I will buy it sight unseen but cannot pick it up because I am in hiding, but if you will drive it to the docks and load it onto a ship I will specify for you we will be most grateful, as my daughter has just been kidnapped. I will instruct dock workers to give you a certified check in the amount of 8714$ that you can purchase the car, send me the title for the car, and then convert the extra into the currency of your country and deposit into the banking institution of your choice.

Thank you and god bless!

The Ferris Wheel

I think I'm in love with him, my reflection said.

The prince? Are you crazy?

We were stopped at the top of the Ferris wheel. The car was swaying on thick cables. The people were tiny, the tops of the trees just below my swinging feet. I was holding my reflection on my lap as I surveyed the spinning scene: Scooterplanes, bumper cars, the ache and groan of the old wooden rollercoaster.

You never did understand me, she said. You thought I was just supposed to follow you around, doing whatever you wanted. And besides, we have a lot in common.

Like what?

We're both unappreciated for one.

I appreciate you.

No you don't. I want to go back.

Back where? There is no back.

You should never have taken me out of the dressing room, she said. I was supposed to be famous.

But this was your idea!

Everything smells like poop and I'm tired of hay in my shoes.

He probably doesn't even really exist.

Oh, like *I* don't really exist?

Just then the Ferris wheel lurched to life and my reflection slipped from my fingers—she plummeted to the concrete and shattered like a small silver bomb.

Let me off! I screamed as I passed the ground—but the teenager controlling the lever shook his head—no can do, you'll have to wait—and the Ferris wheel swooped and lifted and I was back in the treetops as a crowd gathered around the sparkling silver dust.

Then an employee cleared out the crowd and swept my reflection into a dirty pink dustpan, leaving only a cleaned patch of concrete.

Madame C's Hall of Mirrors

I didn't mean it! I shouted, handing over two tickets and pushing through the turnstile. My distorted reflection melted into the moving smears of people and was swallowed by the slight sweat of panic.

Don't lose me! I yelled, feeling my way along the mirrored walls. In the House of Mirrors my body was pulled like taffy and my reflection became wavy and bulging, with an extremely long torso, silly straw legs and a tiny button head. I turned into another dead end and spiraled into a sad corner.

Where are you? I yelled as my reflection curled into a fragmented ball and wouldn't look at me.

The Fortune Teller

The fortune teller looked at my hands, smoothed them onto the table. You lost something, she said.

Yes, I said. I want to get it back.

But you can't get it back, you know that.

That's not true. Don't say that, I insisted. That's why I'm here.

Look, she said, pointing to the fleshy part on the outside of my palm. It's gone. I don't decide these things but I'm telling you what I see.

So what do I do now?

She patted my hand. It's just part of your story, now, she said.

The Bearded Lady

Maybe she went to Mexico, she said. A lot of times they end up in Mexico. Or in the antique stores. Have you checked out all the antique stores? There is an underground market for mirrors, you know, real ones. The ones with actual reflections in them.

If she ended up on the black market I'll never find her, I said.

Not true, said the Bearded Lady. It hasn't actually happened to me, but I've heard of it happening. Things just show up in the black market. Or Mexico. But I'd try the black market first. And wear a disguise, she said. Because if they recognize you, they're gonna charge you double, especially if she's still mad.

I'll be careful.

They're going to try and screw you. Or marry you—be careful of that, too. They'll do anything to get out of there. Don't give anyone your real name. You want me to go with you?

No, I'll be okay, but thanks.

No problem, she said, stroking her beard.

Clown Car

I waited on the side of the highway. There were very few cars passing at this time in the evening and the ones that did switched to the far lane. I was afraid I might be sleeping in the bushes when a car came very slowly, headlights already on, and coasted to a stop in front of me.

I jogged over not too fast not too slow. I saw the window being hand cranked down—the red nose barely visible in the darkening light. Do you have a lot of stuff? he asked.

Just this, I said, holding up my duffel.

Great, he said. Squeeze in wherever you can.

The car smelled like rubber and greasepaint and I squeezed in between two giant sets of feet, a hairy man clown dressed in a diaper, and a mime clown. I could not see out the window at all.

We're planning to drive through the night, the driver clown said, so we'll take turns in the sleeping positions. Every hour someone else has to be in the upside down position because Marty needs a break. And no tricks on the driver.

We puttered through the night that way. Just before dawn I was in one of the sitting up positions watching the way the night lightened until a seam of orange creased the horizon. A golden ball crowned and the morning sky turned rose.

Ah, sighed the clown sitting in my lap, smiling as the sun filled his eyes.

The Ape Lady

Sold to the circus by her parents at the age of nine months, The Monkey Baby grew into The Ape Lady, one of the most famous bearded ladies of all time.

She suffered from congenital hypertrichosis syndrome, a form of excessive hair production that is linked to an abnormality on the X chromosome. Sometimes called Werewolf Syndrome, the same disease is responsible for The Lion Man and The Dogfaced Boy.

The Ape Lady gave birth to The Sword Swallower's child but they both died of complications. The baby had the disorder as well. Overcome with grief, The Sword Swallower had both mother and baby mummified and housed in a German museum, where their bodies were promptly stolen and never recovered.

Maternal Impression

Until the 1900s, *maternal impression* was the popular explanation for a variety of abnormalities and birth defects. The mother of The Elephant Man claimed she was badly frightened by an elephant during her pregnancy. The mother of Lionel the Lion Man claimed she was traumatized after watching her husband get mauled by a lion in her third trimester. Pregnant women were never to look at blind people no matter what.

Clown Sermon

Once I came home from school and my mother was standing in the middle of the living room crying. On the stereo a man was sermonizing:

"And if you play those records backwards, Satan will be speaking to you directly. Some of these so-called performers drink blood during performances." And then he played a record backwards and a very frightening garble came out of the speakers.

Tears carved through my mother's clown makeup.

"Are you willing to say no to Satan and his way into our lives via this music?"

Not knowing what else to do, I stood next to my mother and starting crying too.

She put a big rubber hand on my shoulder and held it there, for comfort.

Clown Porn

Once I found a stash of photographs hidden behind the toilet. Clown wigs but no panties. Clown makeup with bare breasts. Multiple clowns doing things with body parts I'd never even imagined before. I wanted to ask my father about it but I didn't dare.

My Father is Trying to Set a World Record

Why yogurt? I ask.

Because nobody's tried it with yogurt before he says, taking a few warm up breaths.

But I don't get it.

It's about having goals, he says. That's the problem—your mother never taught you the importance of having a real goal.

My Father is Trying to Set the Record for Days Spent Petting a Shark

The trick, he says, is to just lightly move the fingers. The shark has the frozen, unimpressed expression of all sharks.

Are you going to come home for dinner?

I can't stop now, he says. It's only been nine hours. I pet him in different places so he doesn't get a rash. Also I switch hands so my skin doesn't over prune.

Okay, I say. Well I better go.

Don't tell your mother! he shouts as I walk away.

From The Guinness Book of World Records

Longest tongue: 10.1 centimeters

Longest sword swallowed: 58 cm (22.8 inches)

Stretchiest skin: 15 centimeters from body

Farthest arrow shot using feet: 6.09 meters/20 feet

Most apples held in one's own mouth and cut by chainsaw in one minute: 8

Longest time survived trapped underground: 69 days

Most spoons balanced on face: 31

Longest duration of 3 contortionists in a box: 6 min 13.52 seconds

Longest kiss: 58 hours, 35 minutes and 58 seconds

Most people inside of a soap bubble: 214

The World's Longest Fingernails

The world record for the longest fingernails, at 28 ft. 2 inches, was finally set in 2008 after 29 years of growth. One year later the fingernails were all broken in a car accident.

The Black Market

The gypsies watched me with weird eyes. They were decorated and smelled strongly of perfume. The Black Market had a Parisian theme and a hobo clown playing the accordion. I paused in front of a large, old Hollywood mirror with cloudy patches.

What are you looking for? one asked.

I need a new mirror, I said.

He held up a red plastic hand mirror. Mirrors are hard to come by these days, he said. I'm sure you already know that.

That's what I heard, I said. I have something to trade. And when he looked in my bag he said Oh now that is interesting. In that case I might have something that would suit you better. We left out the Exit door where the clowns were smoking in the alley. Says she's looking for a mirror. Anybody know of a mirror that might interest her?

They scrutinized me. One stubbed out a cigarette and said I got a mirror in my trunk. Costs you to look.

He popped the trunk of a gold Plymouth Volare with a broken back window. He tilted up the mirror so I could see into it. The reflection wasn't mine.

Thanks anyway, I said, handing him $20.

My Past Life Self Won't Stop Following Me Around the Museum

She follows me from room to room. Every time I stop to look at a piece, she looks at it too.

Uh-oh.

Uh-oh what?

Oh, nothing.

Look, don't you have anywhere else to be? I ask.

Not really, she says. Where is the portrait room?

Wrong museum, I say.

I've had my portrait painted, she says. Once I posed in the nude.

I stopped. You?

Oh yes, she says. It takes a lot of concentration to stay that still for such a long time, you know. I doubt you could do it.

You're starting to annoy me, I say.

Yes, that's sort of the point, she says, smoothing her hair.

My Clown Mother Has Joined a Cult

And the cult leader says she isn't allowed to talk to any of us, so she's taken to wearing her silent mime costume almost exclusively now, little black stretchy skullcap, black diamond triangles above and below her whitened eyes, sad tear forever falling.

There is one exception: She's allowed to talk to us if we're interested in also joining the cult. So now every time we want to talk to her we have to pretend that we might join the cult. She convinced me to go to one of their meetings—everyone was really nice and offered me lemon bars. I was surprised to see a few other clowns there as well, though none that I recognized.

The cult leader has a day job as a ballroom dance instructor—he teaches cha-cha, foxtrot, rumba, East Coast swing. Sometimes the phone rings late at night and a slurry voice asks for my mother, asks if she was planning on coming to her dance lesson. But we all know what that really means.

My Father is Trying to Beat the Record For Longest Time Without Blinking

Tears are streaming down his face.
Why don't you use your hands? I ask.
It doesn't count if I use my hands, he weeps.

Flea Circus

The first man to harness a flea was a watchmaker in 1509, who used them to demonstrate the inner mechanisms of a watch. By the 1800s, fleas were regularly fitted with permanent gold wires around their necks and attached to tiny circus rides such as chariots, carousels or Ferris wheels. When the fleas jumped they "moved" the contraptions. Sometimes the fleas were glued to the circus ring holding tiny instruments and the floor was heated. As the fleas struggled to escape they appeared to "play" the instruments.

The Human Pincushion

The Human Pincushion, a man named Malaki Jones, could insert knives and swords into his body without any injury or blood loss. Doctors even examined him during his act, confirming that the knives penetrating his body were not harming him.

It's suspected that Jones had created fistulas, or tunnels of scar tissue, by slowly pushing a sharp object inch by inch through his body. As long as something remains inserted in the fistula, the tunnel remains intact. Jones had at least four fistulas that went all the way through; most likely he kept metal rods in the fistulas when not performing so they would not close up.

The year of his death, he claimed to hear voices that told him to swallow a steel needle and then have it surgically removed. He did both, but died of an aortic rupture soon afterwards.

The Augmentation

On her 18th birthday, her mother and grandmother and aunts all sat her down in the good living room. We've been putting money in the fund since you were a baby, they said. We've already talked to Dr. Hill.

But I don't want bigger boobs.

Of course you do, the mother said. The big breasted aunts and the grandma all nodded. And it's better to get them when you're young—ask Diane. Diane's cleavage threatened to swallow her face. Yes, she said. I wish I had done it earlier.

The doctors and nurses were extremely friendly. In the waiting room, other women discussed fat injections, cosmetic skin grafts, voluntary amputations, and how it really doesn't hurt at all to have the lower ribs removed. Most of them agreed that the breast tumors looked more natural than the old implants. On the table, the staff prepped her, and then 10, 9, 8…

When she woke her room was filled with roses and cards. Amidst the stitches and yellow iodine her breasts were two dense dough balls and already swelling. She left with a lifetime prescription for Letrozole meant to keep the tumors from spreading too quickly.

Every two months she had to go in for low-grade radiation treatments. They're filling out nicely, Dr. Hill said, palpating them. No extraneous lumps, growth seems to be happening at the same rate on each side.

One day she was on the train next to a man who was trying not to look at her breasts when she felt a tingling. The breasts began to swell and within minutes they were about to rip through the skin, a meaty fist cracking her ribcage.

She didn't expect the silent looks from the doctors and nurses, who recognized a patient who wasn't going to make it. We thought you'd have more time, they said, shaking their heads like it was her fault.

The Fantasy Hand Job Brothel

Have you ever wanted to get a hand job from George Washington? How about Gandhi, Bette Midler or Don Knotts? Here at the Fantasy Hand Job Brothel, we specialize in making all your fantasy hand jobs come true.

We use the term "hand job" for both our male and female clients, and sexual orientation doesn't bother us. Why hand jobs? Because a hand job is simple and doesn't violate any of the new prostitution codes or spread STDs, and hey, who doesn't want to say they've gotten a hand job from Helen Keller? Keeping everything legal and safe allows you to stop worrying about getting busted and start concentrating on the real task in front of you—getting off.

I started Fantasy Hand Job Brothel 15 years ago when I realized that most "fantasies" were limited to 20 year olds in silky lingerie or sweaty, bare-chested firemen. But what if you secretly desire a hand job from Barry Manilow? What are you to do about it? Hide it away in a shameful place, jerk off to busty blond twins just like the rest of the world?

Don't get me wrong: A classic hand job is a lovely thing, and we have Playboy bunnies and Chippendales and Dallas Cowboy cheerleaders, as well as Marilyn Monroe, James Dean, Elvis Presley, Mae West, and our new two-for-one Brangelina hand job.

But maybe you, like millions of others, secretly want a hand job from Genghis Khan. Or maybe it's Martha Stewart (who also comes as jailbird Martha). The point is, when you want a hand job from Rick Moranis or Oprah Winfrey, we've got it.

Like politics? How about a hand job from FDR or Eleanor Roosevelt? If history is more your thing, try Henry VIII, Marie Curie or Marquis de Sade. Are you a revolutionary? How about a hand job from Angela Davis, Che Guevara, Karl Marx or Malcolm X?

And if you're into philanthropy, what about Mother Teresa?

Still suffering from your childhood religious scarring? We have both skinny and fat Buddha, Mary Magdalene, Joseph Smith and several Hindu gods, including Vishnu and Lakshmi. (Any other god can be designed for you with 48 hours notice.) And if you're on your period, we have a special "Moses Parts the Red Sea" fantasy hand job.

Need a gift for your college graduate? How about a hand job from Albert Einstein? Something special for your mother's 60th birthday? Why not get her that hand job from Tom Selleck that she's always wanted? A unique wedding gift? What about his and hers hand jobs from Romeo and Juliet? Country western fans will be pleased to get our Dolly Parton/Kenny Rogers combo, and the English professor in your life will love our line of literary figures, from Captain Ahab to Alice in Wonderland!

Whatever you can fantasize, we can make it come true.

Upcoming specials:

Gifts of the Magi: Get a hand job complete with gold, frankincense, and myrrh from our own three kings, and during the month of December buy two kings and get the third free.

Luck of the Irish: Want a hand job from a leprechaun? He'll have you kissing the blarney stone and then some.

Kitchen Gourmet: Julia Child will not only give you a great, homemade hand job, but she'll whip up a batch of brownies—with or without nuts.

Beethoven's Birthday Month: Visit Beethoven in December and sing your very own "Ode to Joy!"

On Golden Pond: Celebrate your Golden Anniversary with "Golden" showers on Katharine Hepburn or Henry Fonda...or both!

Beat It: Michael Jackson has one hand in a glove...and the other on you! But hey, the kid isn't *his* son!

New this summer: Satan!

We at Fantasy Hand Job Brothel think everyone is entitled to a good hand job now and then. So from Dionne Warwick to Charlie Chaplin, from Harriet Tubman to Queen Elizabeth, come on down to the Fantasy Hand Job Brothel today and leave satisfied.

- All Fantasy hand job participants must be at least 18 years old.
- Please give 48 hours notice on all specialty hand jobs.
- You may schedule no more than four hand jobs per day for insurance reasons.
- All hand jobs are limited to 30 minutes and results are not guaranteed.

The Talent Agency

I was walking down the street when I finally spotted her—up on the billboard 100 feet high, The Most Famous Woman in the World! Posed up there, with a come-on gaze over one bare shoulder…my reflection.

What the fuck! I thought, mortified. I reached for my can of Instant Fame* and also discovered it missing.

I ran into the nearest Talent Agency—you've made a mistake, I said, pointing to the billboard out the window. I'm the original. She's the reflection!

The secretary smiled at me. I wish I could tell you how many times a day I hear that, she said. Why don't you stand in front of that mirror and prove it?

Oh my! the woman said when a gray haired lady with a bun and a heavy Caribbean accent showed up. Look I had no choice, I said as my temporary reflection mimicked my movements. Do you know how hard it is to put on makeup or even brush your teeth?

Yes, I'm sure it is, she said as she escorted me to the front door and called security.

Stunt Double

You could be her stunt double? the agent suggested.

The Screen Test

We were standing at the edge of a large field. Okay, now everyone listen up. This is a training video for the client so I want you all to act totally natural. Make sure you've all filled out a W-9 if you want to get paid, the guy in the uniform said. And be careful with that mirror—there are absolutely no weapons allowed—you signed that in your release. Okay? Ready? Go!

He shot off the gun.

We stood there unsure.

Go! he yelled again. Run!

Just over the hill I saw the SWAT team coming towards us like big, rippling bears. They had the words SWAT spelled out in white on their black uniforms.

Fuck! someone yelled as we started running.

Don't worry, the checks clear! shouted a guy in a shabby suit.

Singing Telegram

This circus gig is good, The Ringmaster said, but I'm thinking when all this is over I'll probably cut an album or something. I already have a name—*Under My Big Top*. Oh, that reminds me, some of the girls make a little extra money on the side. It's easy and you already have a costume, he said, swirling the ice around in his drink. If you're interested.

Miss July

That's disgusting, my Past Life Self says.

I thought you said you had posed naked. You sounded proud of it.

Yes, but for paintings. That's much different.

I don't see how.

No, you wouldn't, she says, shutting the magazine.

Types of Clowns

The Whiteface/Mime Clown: Also known as Pierrot clowns, these are sad, lovesick clowns that can be verbal or nonverbal. Usually dressed entirely in black and white and wearing a skullcap to cover hair. All exposed skin must be painted white. *See Marcel Marceau*

The Auguste Clown: This is a comedic clown best known for outlandish "antics" and playing tricks on other clowns. Costume should be zany and colorful, with bright wigs (either full or with exposed "bald" crown) and makeup. *See Bozo the Clown, Ronald McDonald*

The Tramp/Hobo Clown: A uniquely American clown, this clown is often the butt of the jokes of the other clowns. Should wear patched rags, shabby, oversized shoes, and have five o'clock shadow with a red, "sunburned" nose. You may add a tear. *See Emmett Kelly, Charlie Chaplin*

Coulrophobia

Coulrophobia, or Clownophobia, is the fear of clowns.

The Pogo Stick

You know other moms don't do that, right? I said, as the spring bounced, bounced, bounced.

My Father Is Trying to Become the Only Living Man with Stigmata

We're at the riverboat casino when it happens. My father bends over and grabs for me as if he's been shot, wipes little bloody handprints on my shoulders. Clear out! the security guards yell as they half carry my father past the poker machines, the black jack tables, the old ladies on the new Batman slots—cover your eyes—you're not old enough to be in the gaming area—up to our hotel room where my father lies sweating on the bed.

It worked! he says once everyone leaves, slowly opening his hands and showing me his palms. It's the stigmata. Two round wounds shimmer with blood but do not drip.

Soon all the maids are knocking at the door, peeking over my shoulder and making the sign of the cross.

Don't tell your mother, he adds as I pull the door shut.

Traveling Medicine Show

Attention men using Testosterone! Did you undergo Testosterone Replacement Therapy and experience blood clots? Heart Attack? Stroke? Cardiac arrest? Pulmonary embolism? Or even death?

Try a swig of Doctor Alaska Jackson's healing nerve tonic and medicinal elixir! Speedy and certain cure!

Attention all men! Do you urinate more? Do you get up in the night to urinate? Do you have a weak or unsteady stream?

Alaska Jackson's healing nerve tonic and medicinal elixir is the remedy! Made with genuine rattlesnake oil from actual shamans!

Have you or your son taken Testosterone Gel and developed female breast tissue?

Try just one spoonful of Alaska Jackson's healing nerve tonic liniment and medicinal elixir plus worm syrup!

Don't ignore the signs of an aging prostate!

Dr. Alaska Jackson's healing medicinal tonic! Nine out of ten people who used Dr. Alaska Jackson's healing nerve tonic and medicinal elixir felt the complete and total elimination of all their symptoms within 48 hours!

You! (He pointed right at me.) Did you or someone you know undergo perforated vaginal scarring when receiving trans-vaginal mesh, which then required an additional surgery to remove the mesh?

You need Dr. Alaska Jackson's healing medicinal elixir ointment and proven hair grower! With extract of wild cherry!

I handed him some money and he handed me a beautiful blue glass corked bottle. *With 87% pure grain alcohol* he said, winking.

Red Ball Infestation

The red balls were everywhere—down the hallways, on the furniture, coating the doorways and doorsills, in the cupboard, crawling into the open cereal boxes. The room was alive and vibrating red balls, the bigger ones sprouting wings. My mother was running around slamming cream pies in her face, vomiting invisible scarves. My father was helplessly eating cheese right out of the fridge.

I don't know whose idea it was to get the imaginary cat, but it took care of all those red balls in just a few hours. Soon shredded tufts of red fuzz covered the floor, a few of the balls still twitching in the hallways.

Cats in the Attic

They're up there. I'm not sure how many. Sometimes when we're eating dinner we'll hear a pounce or a scratchy shuffle above us. We are to never, ever go up there. We have no idea what they would do.

When I can't sleep I'll lay there and listen to their mewling. And some nights after everyone is asleep I climb the stairs to the attic, touching the pink and yellow insulation bulging from the walls. I creak open the door and all the cats turn their heads to look silently at me.

Newspaper Clipping Found in my Father's Things

Wanted: Sideshow Performer. Do you suffer unexplained rashes? Does hair grow all over your body? Are you covered with fish scales? Tattoos? Are you lacking pigmentation? Are you missing vital organs or limbs? Do your knees bend backwards? Do you have the stigmata of Christ? Do you like to travel?

We pay a weekly stipend plus room, board, costuming, and all traveling expenses and best of all you will be in show biz! Exposed to millions across the country and maybe even the world!

Call Madam Velvet's Cabaret of Oddities Now! Auditions taking place soon so don't delay!

The Invisible Girl!

Only visible in reflective surfaces!

For 50 cents you can see the girl who isn't actually there!

The magician towed a full-length mirror covered with a gold velvet cloth onto the stage. She exists—or does she? He whipped off the fabric and there was my stupid reflection in my stolen sparkly costume!

Is she a ghost? the magician asked. Is this a trick?

Two assistants joined him on stage to spin the mirror around. The magician knocked on the back with his knuckles. My reflection had two circles of rouge drawn on her cheeks and tiny red lips like a china doll and she didn't recognize me because I was wearing a disguise.

Money flew through the air. The magician covered the mirror with the fabric again and I heard a slightly muffled cry that was covered by applause.

In the Nightclub Bathroom

A girl was cutting up lines on my reflection's face. Oh, is this what you've been doing? I said as the fat white caterpillar disappeared, leaving traces of dust on her cheek.

Look, I know you can hear me, I said.

Disappearing Ink

After my father left town I found my mother in the bathroom with spirit gum and cotton balls. She'd already removed her floppy clown collar; it left a strange, uneven line where her skin met the white line of greasepaint like ragged fringe on her collarbone. She was swiping a wet cotton ball down her cheek and revealing a zebra stripe of flesh. Her red lipstick eyebrows were permanently stained surprise circles on her forehead. Her black diamond triangle eyes were staring back at her face, her features slaughtered and unrecognizable. Her reflection in the mirror was dripping purple tears. I couldn't watch so I shut the bathroom door.

The Time Capsule II

The Man from the Future arrived to show me where to bury the time capsule. This is going to be really helpful in the future, he said, digging my mother's abandoned clown props out of the dumpster: polka dotted ties, giant flyswatters, powdered whipping cream, cups with red rubber foam balls, a giant hot dog with giant pickles, squirting cigarettes, disappearing ink, a tiny finger guillotine, a giant pacifier, diaper and bonnet from under the old coffee grounds.

We stuffed all these things in an old metal garbage can and he led me to the spot. So much has been paved over in the future, he said. This little strip of dirt is all that's left.

Future Self

I was backstage. The crowd was applauding. I peeked through the heavy maroon curtains and there was my Future Self in the spotlight. She saw me and her face opened like a flower to the sun.

I walked on stage and sat next to her. Then I noticed I was sitting in a chair labeled "Before" as the audience clapped and whistled.

Chain Letter

Congratulations on having received this letter. This is one of the longest lasting chains ever recorded so do not break it. You must send a baby you have birthed yourself to the next woman on the list. And then in 8-10 days you will receive babies from all over the world! You should send these babies UPS or FedEx only, with tracking numbers. Be sure to poke holes in the box and it's recommended that you line the box with something absorbent like shredded newspapers or maybe dishtowels. Some people like to give a sedative to the baby. If you meet in person it should not be in a public area and you should avoid words like "baby" or "box".

Please provide a current address. Erase the last woman's name from the top of this list and add yours when you send your baby. This chain has been going on for 35 years so DON'T BREAK IT.

With love!!

The Escort

I'm not going to sleep with you for money, she said right away when I opened the door. She was wearing mint green nurse's scrubs with little suns and moons on them. I just came from work and decided not to dress up so you wouldn't get the wrong idea.

We were silent in the taxi. She yawned and pulled out baby wipes and wiped her hands, then the door handles, then offered one to me. When I refused she insisted—it's antibacterial, she said. You never know who sat in this cab before you. Where are we going?

How about a nice steak?

I'm a vegan, she said. But everyone wants a steak so I'm used to it.

Listen, I said. I'm trying to make someone jealous here, so maybe when we get there you could hang on me a little? Pretend you're really into me?

At the restaurant the hostess seated us far in the corner. Tom Selleck was seated a few tables away with a woman who was smoking a cigar and the whole restaurant was a-chatter. As we passed the bar I saw my reflection watching from the glass behind all the bottles. Not smiling.

My escort removed a paper bag from her purse and set it neatly to the side.

So, how long have you been doing this?

Nursing?

No, escorting.

Oh that. A while. It's mostly old men so this is a nice change. I got to see *Cats* last weekend.

How was it?

Dumb. She was unwrapping a Subway sandwich on her salad plate. I'll order some fries to go with this.

I'm sure they can make you a fresh sandwich?

No, this is just easier. You want to talk about current events or something? I read the paper.

Not really. Tell me something about you.

Oh no, let's not go there.

When my steak came along with her plate of fries she excused herself and didn't come back for 20 minutes. Sorry, she said when she returned. I had to throw up. I'm fine now. She rummaged through her purse for a breath mint. I feel much better.

Outside the restaurant I tried to hail a cab but she backed away. Oh no, she said. I already told you I'm not sleeping with you.

I'm just getting a cab.

Maybe you better just pay me now and I'll take the bus, she said as the #15 pulled up to the curb. I handed her some money and the doors whooshed closed behind her.

Vertigo

What you're suffering from is just a classic case of vertigo, the doctor said.

But I'm not afraid of heights.

Vertigo is a fear of *falling*, not heights. This is not a Hitchcock movie, the doctor said, snapping off her gloves. Maybe if you quit standing up this wouldn't happen.

I shouldn't stand up at all?

It depends on how badly you want this dizziness to pass, the doctor said. But I would certainly recommend standing as little as possible. I can get you a second opinion if you like she added, opening the door and shouting to the receptionist.

The receptionist joined us in the examination room. I was telling our patient here that if she wants to stop feeling dizzy she needs to just stay on the floor at all times. She wants a second opinion.

Well that sounds perfectly reasonable to me, the receptionist said, as the phone rang and called her back to her desk.

Plan B

Maybe this is a blessing, the therapist said. There are plenty of other reflections out there—you could have any reflection you wanted. Or maybe it's even time to go solo.

She squeezed my hand. You know, I wasn't going to mention this, but it's really no big deal to make her disappear, if you wanted. I know a doctor who'll do it. Break the mirror and scatter the pieces, if you know what I mean. A little rearranging, if you catch my drift.

The Death of Harry Houdini

Harry Houdini began his escape routine as Harry "Handcuff" Houdini on the vaudeville circuit, but soon he was escaping from straitjackets, chains, hanging from skyscrapers, buried alive, and from the back of a Siberian prison transport van. He escaped from nailed packing crates, riveted boilers, a barrel filled with beer, and even the belly of a whale that had washed up on the beach. His most famous act, the Chinese Water Torture Cell, had Houdini lowered upside down into a locked glass and steel cabinet overflowing with water and holding his breath up to 3 minutes while escaping.

A week before his death two men broke into Houdini's dressing room, yelling "Do you believe in the miracles of the Bible?" while repeatedly punching him in the gut. He died of a ruptured appendix a week later.

The Last Human Zoo

The 1955 "Missing Link" exhibit at the Bronx Zoo, touted as "an exhibit in genetics and the evolution of the species", was open for only 48 hours. The anthropologist who designed and organized the exhibit, which included pygmies and "tribals" hired in exchange for passage to the U.S., displayed the people next to monkey cages where the public could view and see "the missing link" in the evolutionary chain.

After two days of record-breaking attendance the exhibit was shut down. The people who were exhibited were found wandering the empty zoo grounds, confused, frightened, and yelled at by spectators from behind the gates.

The Last Leper Colony

The last known leper colony still exists high in the mountains of Romania. A cure for leprosy was discovered in the 1950s, but for the advanced cases the cure only made them not contagious. The last leper colony in Romania houses less than 20 residents, most of them elderly. Even though they are free to leave, nobody does. Many of the residents have spent their entire lives there and report being afraid of "losing pieces of themselves" if they were to leave.

The One Thing My Grandfather Won't Talk About

When my 17-year-old grandfather arrived with the other American soldiers to liberate Dachau, they found the gates unlocked, the sniper towers deserted. The Nazis had abandoned the camp a week before. For more than a week the prisoners had no idea they were free.

The Brother and Sister

The brother and sister tried to pass it off but everyone knew. The way they both avoided certain subjects. The way the other's skin had felt like it was on fire, familiar like childhood. The way they had held each other, frightened afterwards.

Rod Stewart at Skate City

He's wearing a maroon jogging jacket and pants and his hair is swept over his tan forehead. Now he leans over the railing while I circle the rink, staring. Now he helps a kid with his skates. Now he drinks a Blue Raspberry Slushie. When the announcer calls for adult skate, Rod Stewart ventures onto the floor, wobbling and then steadying himself.

Why is no one else reacting? That's *Rod Stewart!* I confirm his identity from other angles—the long nose and profile with a hint of a point, the back of the hair brushing the collar. He looks sad, circling the rink—who remembers Da Ya Think I'm Sexy? Certainly not those 8 year olds in leopard print leggings. I watch his frosted hair until I finally lose him in the shadows.

Most Urgent Telegram of All

Dear Miss,

Thank you for the picture you send—you look exactly like Liza Minnelli. I cannot wait to meet you. We have beaches and I have an empty bungalow on the beach. Here is a satisfying picture of it. You will look so beautiful there. Might I ask you a small favor until then? I would be most grateful if you would meet me at the docks with your can of Instant Fame*—I may not have much longer to live, but I think I might be in love with you as well. Please bring your social security card with you and my heart cannot stop beating at the sight of meeting your person.

~Yours

The Face Lift

I just can't look at her anymore, I said.

That's usually the case, the doctor said. Feel betrayed?

Sort of.

Do you want revenge or do you want to disappear?

What's the difference?

Well if you want to disappear then we change you quite a bit, really mess you up. But if you want revenge then we only do a little tweak here and there…just enough. Every now and then I give a facelift so subtle that I actually feel bad when I catch the old reflection sniffing around later. Heartbreaking. You have to really want revenge to go that route.

Or I can give you a nice celebrity-style botched job—guaranteed to make you unrecognizable, even to yourself. Good if you want to do some spying and such.

I might need to think about it.

I would, he said. Because all facelifts are nonrefundable and I'm not obligated to do any follow up work if I don't like your face.

Interview with The Electric Lady

I was hit by lightening as a child in Kansas, she said. That was the official story. I'd come on stage and the lights would flicker and my hair would stand on end and stuff.

Oh, I did all sorts of things. I was also Irene the Iron Tongued Girl—I had my tongue pierced with an iron rod. I was the Lizard Skin Woman for awhile. I was supposed to have this lizard skin that stretches.

Well, you see, people are funny. They believe what they want to believe. If they're expecting to see something, if they're told they're going to see something, then they see it.

No, of course it wasn't real. I would never pierce my tongue for $50 a week.

The Incredible Shrinking Woman

I'm growing while she's shrinking. Every day she's getting so small. Pretty soon I'm afraid we're going to have to say goodbye.

The Ringmaster

I found The Ringmaster sneaking out late one night with a bunch of Nembutal in his bag. What is this? I asked.

It's medicine used by vets, he said.

Are you a vet? I said.

No, he said.

Then what do you plan to do with all this Nembutal?

He looked away. I didn't make it onto the reality television show, he said.

Don't you know those shows are rigged to humiliate you in front of a national audience?

It doesn't matter now, he said. I didn't get on. They said I was on and then they changed their minds or something. Look, he added, it would be great if you wouldn't mention this to anyone, he said, carefully closing and latching the suitcase on crumpled dollar bills and heading for the train station.

Condemned

The guys in Hazmat suits came on a Wednesday. You're going to have to clear out, they said. This place is full of asbestos.

What? You can't just walk in and do that.

Oh yes, yes we can, they said. Infested with it. Hopefully you won't all grow up deformed or something.

The Mirage

I smelled smoke and flipped on the bathroom light and there she was, my reflection, cigarette in hand, spraying Lysol from behind the spotted motel mirror.

Oh, so you're back now?

She rolled her eyes. What happened to your face?

Our face, I said. I made some changes.

You look like shit.

Thanks, I said. What happened to Mr. Gold Bars?

I don't want to talk about it.

Where's my can of Instant Fame*?

That's gone, she said. It didn't work anyway.

Acknowledgements

I'm especially grateful to my early readers Sally Reno, Rob Geisen, Kona Morris, James Thomas and Len Kuntz; also to everyone at the Fbomb Flash Fiction Reading Series, who were my "early listeners" for many of these pieces.

I've been supported by and collaborated with so many amazing people and organizations, including Patricia Morrison, Kathy Fish, Paul Beckman, Meg Tuite, Robert Vaughan, Jonathan Montgomery, Bryan Jansing, David S. Atkinson, Robert Scotellaro, Jonathan Cardew, Jayne Martin, Grant Faulkner, Lynn Mundell, Pamela Painter, Robert Shapard, Leah Rogin-Roper, Monique Antonette Lewis, Nick Morris, Steven Dunn, Travis Cebula, Sharon Busheff, Erik Wilkins, Scott Ryplewski, Mayra Walters, Rory Reagan, Beyond Academia, the Bath Flash Fiction Festival, Bending Genres, *Blink Ink*, The International Flash Fiction Association, The Denver Lit Crawl, The Mercury Café, and all my talented colleagues in academia.

Thank you to Susan Ryplewski for the beautiful cover art.

To Robin Stratton and Becky LeJeune and for the special guidance of Mitch Rosacker.

And lastly to Maiya and Felix and to the Ringmaster Nick Busheff: early reader, early listener, cheerleader, and collaborator, who has created music to and performed over a dozen of these pieces with me.

About the Author

Nancy Stohlman is the author of many books including the flash fiction collection *The Vixen Scream and Other Bible Stories*, *The Monster Opera, Searching for Suzi: a flash novel*, and *Fast Forward: The Mix Tape,* which was a finalist for a 2011 Colorado Book Award. Dubbed "Flash Fiction's Poster Girl" by the hip *Westword* weekly, she is the creator and curator of The Fbomb Flash Fiction Reading Series, the creator of FlashNano in November, and the co-founder of Flash Fiction Retreats, among others endeavors. Her work has been published in over 100 journals and anthologies including the WW Norton anthology *New Micro: Very Short Stories* and has been nominated for a Pushcart Prize. She lives in Denver and teaches at the University of Colorado Boulder. Find out more about her at www.nancystohlman.com.